The First Time Investor

HOW TO INVEST WITH LITTLE MONEY

BRUCE WALKER

Copyright © 2019 by Bruce Walker
All Rights Reserved

Disclaimer:

No part of this publication may be reproduced or transmitted in any form or by any means, or transmitted electronically without direct written permission in writing from the author.

While all attempts have been made to verify the information provided in this publication, neither the author nor the publisher assumes any responsibility for errors, omissions, or misuse of the subject matter contained in this eBook.

This eBook is for entertainment purposes only, and the views expressed are those of the author alone, and should not be taken as expert instruction. The reader is responsible for their own actions.

Adherence to applicable laws and regulations, including international, federal, state, and local governing professional licensing business practices, advertising, and all other aspects of doing business in the U.S.A, Canada or any other jurisdiction is the sole responsibility of the purchaser or reader.

Contents

Introduction 1
  Peak performance relies on investing in 4 separate, but related areas of human well-being: mental, emotional, physical and spiritual. 10
  Defining your purpose 12
  Identifying where you are right now 15
  Taking Action is the key.......................................16

The Timing and Risk of Investing....................... 19

Investing your way to financial independence 31
  The power of investing in Bonds........................32
  Passive Investing...38

Conclusion... 44

**Bonus- The Smart Passive Income
    (Chapter 1-2) Introduction 47**

Chapter 1: Do what Successful people do 52
    What is Passive Income? 53
    Who Can Make Passive Incomes? 56
    How Successful People Make
    Passive Incomes 57

Chapter 2: The Truth about Passive Income 67
    Common Misconceived Thoughts
    about Passive Income 68
    The Reality of Making Passive Income 73

Introduction

When it comes to investing, most people immediately start thinking about money.

Standard, most popular definition of investing is:

Investing is the act of spending money or capital in an endeavor (a business, project, real estate, etc.) with the expectation of gaining a profit or additional income.

A lot of books on investing are devoted exactly to this topic. They talk about certain businesses and certain ventures that are supposed to make you money.

What you will often find after reading such books is that an author would describe a particular scenario, tricks or a way of doing things that worked for him or her in his or her situation, but isn't applicable to you at all.

This book talks about investing in a broader sense.

Devoting time, effort, energy to a certain area of life, project or even a relationship can also be viewed as investing. When we are young, we invest time in going to school and doing homework. Later we invest energy into work and relationships. As we get older, we start to actually invest money to save for retirement. No matter what age a person is, it is always a smart idea to invest in health, sleep well, eat quality foods and exercise.

We will first outline the areas of life you should be investing in and then will talk about when in your life you should invest in what.

In your 20s you are young and most likely don't yet have a family. This is not the time for conservative long-term investments, even though we do mention a few that are worth pursuing even in your 20s. This is the time to travel, explore mini-retirements and take risks.

In your 30s, 40s, and 50s you are more likely to be making more money than you have been in your 20s.

As you approach retirement age, you need to start becoming more conservative in your financial investments.

One of the main questions people have about retirement is the following: Do I have enough money to retire? Will I be able to live comfortably using my savings? The lifespan of people in the Western World is constantly increasing. You will live longer than you planned. This is good news. However, it is also bad news, because a long life requires a great deal of planning.

Today out of workers fifty-five and older only one person out of four has invested assets of more than $100,000. One in three has less than $50,000. One out of every two baby boomers will not have enough savings to stay at their pre-retirement standard of living. Nearly two of four boomers say that they are not confident they will outlive their savings.

Later in this book, we will also discuss the subject of how much you need to save for retirement and give you tips on how much you need to save in order to live comfortably once you stop working.

Finally, we will discuss investment strategies that you can use in the long run during your entire life. These strategies are based on a number of principles.

The first principle is that your profession and career are most likely to be the main source of your investable assets. Financial investing can be very powerful in growing your money, but in order to start investing, you need money, to begin with. This money is most likely to come from your job or your business and not some crazy stock trade or a lottery win. It is much more important to focus on making a stable reasonable amount of money than to chase non-existent opportunities. Financial investing should not be a process that takes your money and puts it into really risky arrangements.

Secondly, you should never assume that you'd be able to replace your assets. Some people think that they'll be able to earn back money lost in bad investments. This is simply not true. If you lose a large investment, it can take years and even decades of hard work to replace it. When losses of this size occur, investors often find that it is literally impossible to replace them no matter how long they work or how much they additionally save. Remember, as you get older, you are not getting faster or healthier. Taking huge risks with money you saved is gambling and gambling is never a smart idea.

Thirdly, this book is about investing, not speculating. Investing is a process of defining a goal and executing a strategy that will take you to your goal. Focus and emphasis are on long-term results. Speculating is a process of engaging in financial activities for short-term profits, looking for the next big shiny thing, hot stock ideas, day trading or other highly risky approaches.

Principle number four is that no one knows what will happen in the future. Most people wouldn't go to a psychic every day to get a prediction about that day and advice on how they should behave. The idea of doing this every day sounds comical.

At the same time, these same people gladly listen to talking heads on TV that love dispensing advice, including financial investment advice. Most of these TV prognosticators are wrong the majority of the time and it is easy to check this fact, but it seems that no one ever does. If someone really knew what would happen tomorrow, why are they on TV? Even if they could make 10% on their investment daily, they could have started with a $1 and be billionaires very quickly.

The final rule is that no one can time the market. If you follow some investment guru long enough, you will find that he or she makes some good suggestions and some bad ones. Very few people can reliably beat the market consistently over time. Market timing doesn't work. It doesn't matter who tells you that it does or how scientifically correct their arguments sound. If market timing worked, everybody would be doing it.

This is why in this book you will not find a magic pill, only proven, reliable strategies that work over and over again.

The Truth About Investing

As we discussed in the introduction, most people think that investing is only about money. They are sure that the only way to become an investor is to work really hard, make a lot of money working for someone or maybe start their own business and then they get to invest.

The problem with this way of thinking is that in most cases it doesn't result in success.

The biggest issue that is wrong with this approach is that it is impossible to focus just on work or making money or investing money.

Need an example? Just look at the people around you.

Most people are trying really hard to do the best they can. They race through their lives without pausing in an attempt to do and accomplish as much as possible.

They forget to stop and consider who they really are, what they really want and where they really want to go in life. They are wired with smartphones and other devices that are supposed to make them more productive and in control, but inside they are melting down.

When someone works as much as they can to make as much money as they can, demand soon starts to exceed capacity. The next step is getting very little sleep, eating fast foods on the run, fueling up with coffee and unwinding with alcohol and sleeping pills. In today's world words like crazy, obsessed and overwhelmed are used not to describe insanity, but to talk about a typical day.

Feeling that they have no time, people try to stick as much as possible into every day, but often find that it doesn't work.

You need to approach your life in a different way.

If you want to invest money, it is probably because you want to make money to be able to enjoy engaging in activities you want and having the things you want. Most likely, you want to stay healthy, so that by the time you have the money, your health would allow you to enjoy it.

You also want to have friends, to build and sustain relationships. Making a lot of money, but being completely alone probably doesn't sound fun, either.

To sum this up, you are looking to be able to be engaged, emotionally positive and be able to perform, whatever it may mean to you.

Performance, just like investing, has a lot of meanings. You may want to perform at work to climb the career ladder. Or maybe you want to travel a lot and visit a lot of countries. This also is performance.

How do you reach your peak performance levels? What do you need to invest in order to become your best self?

There is an example right in front of our eyes. This example is professional athletes. Most of them reach, sustain and grow their performance levels. The key, therefore, is to look at what they do and then transfer the principle to the things that are important to you.

The key to accomplishment, health, and happiness lie in the skillful management, investment, and replenishment of energy.

Without knowing how to manage energy professional athletes simply wouldn't be professional athletes. They won't be able to be at their peak when they compete and won't be able to win any competitions or races.

Professional athletes spend 90% of their time training in order to be able to perform at their peak for about 10% of the time. Their entire lives are built on creating, sustaining and renewing energy that they need to compete during the relatively short period of time.

On a practical level, this means building routines and rituals to manage energy in all aspects of their lives – sleeping and being awake, working out, resting and eating, getting and staying focused on the mission and goals that they've set for themselves.

Most people, probably including you, spend very little time training in these dimensions, yet we are expected to be at your peak 8, 10, 12 times a day.

Here's another thing that athletes do that most people don't do: professional athletes take the time to recharge. They have an off-season that lasts four to five months a year. For several months, they compete under intense pressure. Then they take the time to rest, renew, heal and grow.

What about you? Your "off-season" probably lasts a few weeks a year at most.

Even during the supposed off-time, most people are busy running errands or staying in touch with the office to make sure things at work are going smoothly.

Given these unpleasant facts, what do you need to invest in to be able to keep performing, enjoy life, be able to make money and have a great time spending money?

Peak performance relies on investing in 4 separate, but related areas of human well-being: mental, emotional, physical and spiritual.

In order to be successful and achieve what you want out of life, you need to invest in all these areas.

We, humans, are complex beings. Happiness is not one-dimensional. We have different needs and different kinds of energy flowing through us.

Subtract development in any one of these areas of life from the equation and your capacity to engage, produce and enjoy life will be significantly reduced, much in the same way an engine misfires when one of the cylinders isn't tuned up properly.

Physical is usually measured in terms of quantity, low to high. Emotional is measured in quality, negative to positive. These two areas are the primary ones because without them functioning properly something will be missing.

For example, you may make a lot of money if you are depressed (depression means negative emotional quality), but you won't be able to enjoy it in this emotional state.

The importance of these areas of life is described best in situations where the consequences of something missing are the most profound.

Imagine that you are having an open-heart surgery. What emotions do you want your surgeon to have? You probably want him or her to be calm, cool and collected. The same goes for the physical state. Most likely, you want a doctor in the best health possible. You don't want someone with shaking hands, tired, running on not enough sleep.

How can you build and sustain success in all four areas of life, especially taking into consideration that the demands in our lives get bigger and our capacity gets smaller with age?

Making investments that last is a three-step process.

The first step is to define the purpose.

The second step is to identify where you are.

The third step is to take action that will take you from where you are to your purpose.

Defining your purpose

Humans are creatures of habit. We often get stuck doing things we know aren't useful for us.

You need the inspiration to create change in your life. Think about the following questions:

1. What are my deepest values?
2. What and how should I invest in to be consistent with my deepest values?

The problem with today's high speed over the communicated way of life is that we rarely stop to reflect on our deepest values. The absence of such reflection, in its turn, makes it hard to keep priorities front and center. Instead of doing the things that matter most to us and making conscious choices about our own priorities, we often spend time reacting to distractions and demands imposed on us by others.

In this stage, your goal is to create a vision for yourself in all four most areas of life that we mentioned.

What you think about yourself today is built on what you remember about yourself in the past. Your memories consist of pictures that you have in your mind. These pictures of you in the past grew out of how you interpreted your past experiences.

You can use the same method to build a new vision for yourself. You can decide on what kind of person you want to be and what experiences you want to have and then imagine the pictures and place them in your mind.

Set a period of half an hour a day when you can be completely uninterrupted. Relax and make yourself comfortable. Close your eyes and use your imagination. Create motion pictures of yourself the way you'd like to be in the future. The key is to make these pictures as detailed as possible. The way to accomplish this is to pay attention to small details, such as sounds, sights, objects in the environment you are imagining.

Details are important because you are creating a practice experience. If your imagination is vivid, your brain will treat this imaginary experience as an actual experience as far as your nervous system is concerned.

This exercise will build new memories into your midbrain. It will help you realize what and who you want to become in the future.

If it is hard for you to identify what you want, you can go the opposite route: decide on what you don't want. What kind of person do you absolutely not want to be? You can start by describing that person. Next, ask yourself about what this person is doing in order to be the way he or she is. The final step is to do the opposite of what this person is doing.

Now you know what kind of person you want to become and what areas of life you should be investing in. This is your destination point.

It is impossible to get to a destination if you do not know where you are currently located. Let's say you need to drive to New York. If you are in Miami, you'll need to drive north. If you are in Boston, you'll need to drive south.

This is why you need to honestly look at who you are today. This is where the next stage of the process comes to help.

Identifying where you are right now

The question you should ask yourself is: "What am I doing about physical, mental, spiritual and emotional areas of my life right now?"

We all regularly underestimate the consequences of the choices we make.

Physical:

What foods are you currently eating?

How much alcohol are you currently consuming?

Do you exercise on a regular level?

Too often we live with rose-colored glasses on, seeing ourselves as victims and coming with excuses for why we are making choices that have a serious negative impact on the quality of our lives.

Identifying where you begin with collecting specific data. Take a blood test, write down what you eat for a few days, keep track of how much you exercise and how much sleep do you get.

Speaking of your emotional well-being,

Do you have a high level of positive emotions in your life?

How do you respond to emotional confrontations?

How do you accept the criticism and opinions of others that you don't agree with?

Here are some questions that will help you understand where you are mentally:

Can you sustain attention for long periods of time?

Are you capable of unplugging so that distractions such as emails do not interrupt you?

Spiritual questions:

Are you honest with yourself even on difficult and sensitive issues?

Are you guided more by your vision and purpose or by external challenges?

Do your behavior and the things that you say at work and at home reflect your inner purpose?

Are you selective about what activities you engage in and where you invest your time and energy?

Taking Action is the key

Here you want to close the gap between the person you want to become and the person you are. This step involves building a life investment plan. You want to create rituals that you engage in on a regular basis.

Examples include

- throwing out junk food and replacing it with healthy eats

- cutting out alcohol and smoking and instead investing in your health by joining a gym or yoga studio

- setting aside challenging projects of today and investing time in long-term projects that are in tune with your purpose

- investing some time in your studies, education and reading to build up your mental capacity

- building new habits and investing in new things requires very specific behaviors and performing them at very specific times.

If you haven't been to a gym for a while and you simply decide that "you need to go to the gym," chances are that nothing will happen. Here's how you need to talk to yourself: "I will go to the gym located at such and such address on Mondays, Wednesdays, and Fridays between 6 pm and 7 pm every week. In order to accomplish this task, I need to buy 2 pairs of athletic sneakers and activewear. I will do so on such and such a day at this very time."

Physical, Spiritual, Mental, Emotional. Identify where you want to be in all these areas of life. Figure out what you need to get there and do it!

The Timing and Risk of Investing

In the previous chapter, we talked about 4 areas of life you should be investing your time, energy and other resources. These areas are physical, emotional, mental and spiritual. These areas are the backbone of your well-being. Investing in them is also risk-free.

When you exercise and improve your health, the benefits of being healthy will stay with you for a long time. When you read, attend seminars, invest in your education and learn, that's also risk-free because nobody can take knowledge away from you.

In this chapter, we will discuss investing at different ages and also start discussing financial investments.

If you are 18 to 30 years old, you may be going to school. It is possible that you are on your first or second job and are considering marriage and a family.

You need to understand that most of the money you make during your life will come from your profession and work. It is true that financial investment can be very lucrative and can grow your money, but it's normally your job that provides the money that you can invest.

We all see stories on TV about people winning a billion-dollar Powerball, a multi-million dollar lottery or suddenly becoming millionaires because of some weird IPO. It is easy to get distracted by such stories.

However, the reason journalists talk about these stories is because they are so rare. It is much more important to focus on making money with your profession and become as productive and prolific as possible in it.

Holding a hope of making a 10,000% return on investment in a short period of time is not the brightest of ideas. Financial investing should be a process of taking your earnings and allowing them to grow somewhat safely. It should not be a process similar to going to a casino and gambling your money on risky bets.

This is why in your 20s it makes sense to invest in a great education and spend time becoming really good at what you do.

Getting started is the hardest thing there is. If you have your first job and you are great at it, it will be easier for you to get great references and find an even better job, should you decide to do so. It will also give you confidence because you will know what you are good at.

However, even if you are really focused on your job, do not forget about the four areas of life and taking a break now and then.

In his book "The 4 Hour Workweek", Tim Ferris introduced the idea of a mini-retirement. A mini-retirement means relocating to one place for a period of one to six months before moving back home or to another location.

A mini-retirement is not an escape from your regular life. It is a creation of a blank slate. Rather than experiencing a vacation through a photo lens and Instagram, a mini-retirement can help you see the world at a speed that is suitable for you and discover things about yourself that you wouldn't be able to see in a regular surrounding or during a one-week trip somewhere.

If you are in your early 20s – 30s, you probably don't have a family yet. Therefore it's a great time for mini-retirements.

Will your employer allow you to work remotely for some period of time? If the answer is yes, you could move and experience a different state, city or country. Did you decide to get a new job? Again, you could travel and try finding work elsewhere, at least for a short period of time.

Freedom is much more than having a lot of money and time to do what you want. It is possible to have both time and money and still be stuck in a hamster's wheel. The time to experiment, find your favorite place to live, see things you want to see, and backpack through Europe are in your 20s. Take advantage of it!

Before we discuss financial decisions for young adults, we need to cover the concept of risk. Risks exist in almost everything you do. However, some risks are more visible and obvious than others.

Oftentimes the risks you are hearing about on TV and reading in newspapers are minimal. The reason these risk and events are featured in the news is the same why mega million lottery winners are on the news, these events are extremely rare. Yet a lot of these events are very memorable and people make incorrect assumptions about them.

For example, most people who are afraid of flying on planes simply do not realize that flying on a plane is much safer than riding in a car.

In 1990, 500 million airline passengers flew an average distance of 800 miles in the US. There have been more than 7 million takeoffs and landings that occurred in all kinds of weather conditions. 39 lives were lost. This same year the National Transportation Safety Board reported that over 46,000 people were killed in car accidents. This means that a person is about 40 times more likely to die in a car than in an airplane.

This doesn't mean that you shouldn't drive or fly. This being said, you may consider taking steps that reduce the risk of injury in your car, such as buying a car with extra security features. Avoiding reckless drivers on highways also diminishes the risks of getting into an accident while driving.

You need to find a golden middle between "fun" risks (such as skydiving without having active health insurance) and life with absolute minimal risks. Most people would easily acknowledge that they would be less happy living a completely riskless life, which isn't even possible in the first place.

Likewise, financial investments also are associated with risks. If you were to try and avoid all the risks of investing, you'd probably not succeed and you won't be happy with the results such riskless investments provide.

Life does not exist without risk. Risk-free activities do not exist. You can minimize risk, but you can't avoid it completely. Different types of investments come with different kinds of risk.

For example, although the stock market is great for long-term investments, it can also drop significantly in a very short time. After peaking in 2000, US stocks on the S&P 500 list dropped by about 50% by 2002. Stocks on the NASDAQ during the same period of time plunged more than 76%.

In six weeks from July 1998 to September 1998 stocks of large companies in the US fell about 20%.

This is where diversification comes into play. In finance, diversification is the process of allocating capital in a way that reduces one particular kind of risk. A common way to diversify is to invest in a variety of different assets.

These assets may include stocks, bonds, gold, real estate, investing in a small business, collectibles, lending investments and so on.

What should you invest in? This depends on your risk tolerance.

Risk tolerance is the degree of variability in investment returns that an individual is willing to withstand. It is a very important component of investing. You should have a realistic view of your ability and willingness to deal with large changes in the value of your investments.

You can identify your risk tolerance by taking a risk tolerance test online. A lot of such tests are free. In addition, it is always useful to review worst-case scenarios for your investments.

A lot of people tend to focus only on the positive and are completely unprepared for the negative turns of events. This is not a smart approach to investing. You always want to take a look at the worst-case scenario and ask yourself if you are willing to deal with it.

Other factors that influence risk tolerance include the time horizon for investing, the presence of other assets and future earnings capacity.

As we've discussed above, it is likely that you have more freedom in your 20s than you will have at other stages of your life. Also, most people in their 40s and 50s make way more money compared to people in their 20s. This is why the 20s are a great time to pursue aggressive investment opportunities such as domestic equity funds, investing in real estate and in foreign markets.

This being said, individual retirement accounts, such as Roth IRA or Traditional IRA, and employer-based plans such as 401k are always a smart choice. These plans are designed to fund your retirement and allow you to make contributions or withdrawals to your retirement savings tax-free.

The abbreviation IRA stands for Individual Retirement Account. Roth IRA was established in 1997 and was named for its main legislation sponsor, Senator William Roth of Delaware.

An IRA account can contain investments in securities and mutual funds. Notes, certificates of deposit and even real estate are also sometimes possible.

Anyone younger than 70.5 years of age with an earned income can make a contribution to his or her regular IRA. Roth IRAs have income eligibility restrictions. For example, in 2015 in order to qualify for Roth IRA, a single taxpayer had to have an adjusted gross income of less than $131,000.

Traditional IRAs are tax-deductible on for both state and federal tax purposes for the years you make a contribution. Withdrawals from IRAs at retirement age are taxed at regular income tax rates. Roth IRAs have no tax break for contributions, but withdrawals are usually tax-free.

To sum up, with regular IRAs you don't pay taxes when you invest the money. With Roth IRAs, you don't pay taxes when you take the money out of retirement.

A 401k is a retirement savings plan sponsored by your employers. Its name comes from the section of the tax code that describes such plans. Here's how it works: your employer would deduct a portion of your paycheck before taxing you and deposit the money into a separate account. Sometimes an employer would match the funds that you choose to deduct. In 2015 maximum pre-tax annual contribution was $18,000.

Let's now talk about investment strategies in your 30s and 40s. If you are in this age bracket, there's a high probability that you are married and have a family. You are probably making more money than you've been making in your 20s. You are also getting closer to retirement.

Investing in your health and positive emotional well-being should still be priorities. However, your financial investment strategies do need to change.

A smart strategy includes maximizing contributions to your IRAs and 401k. You may also want to consider entering the stock market, which allows for greater control and diversification of your assets.

Despite the increased income, a rule of thumb is to be more conservative as you get older.

A lot of people in the United States spend all the money they make on things they don't need and end up broke. That's not where you want to end up. While a lifestyle of spending everything you make may sound tempting at the moment, but it's a recipe for a disaster.

According to an article on MarketWatch.com from December of 2015, over 20% of Americans don't even have a savings account. Approximately 62% of

Americans have less than $1,000 in savings. They say that faced with an emergency, they'd borrow from family, use a credit card or reduce spending elsewhere. Doesn't sound like fun, does it?

Out of the remaining 38% who do have savings, only 14% have a balance of $10,000 or more in their savings accounts.

This all means a very simple thing: you can't base your investment decisions and strategies based on what the majority is doing. You want to find people who are proven successful experts and follow them.

At this age, you should also consider investing in bonds and government-backed securities. These investment vehicles provide solid returns and liquidity should you need to convert your investment assets into cash.

When you get to retirement age, your strategies should change yet again. The main goal should consist of the preservation of wealth and the creation of a level of income that you'll need to maintain a specific lifestyle.

By the time you reach retirement, you would have spent decades saving and investing your hard-earned money. Retirement is the time to use these savings and investments for a living, healthcare, recreation, traveling and your hobbies.

The 4% rule is one of the most popular rules when it comes to finances and retirement. It says that you shouldn't take more than 4.5% of your savings annually after you stop working. If you stick with this rule, your savings will last for at least 30 years of retirement.

This rule is great for planning how much money you need to save to comfortably retire. Make a budget of all your annual expenses in retirement based on the lifestyle you'd like to have. Next, multiply this amount by 25. That's how much money you need to have in savings in order to be able to retire the way you want.

Investing your way to financial independence

In the previous chapter, we discussed investing in different stages of life. We discussed in detail strategies that are appropriate for any age, such as saving money with IRAs, Roth IRAs, and 401k contributions.

In this chapter, we will discuss a safe approach to investing that you can use when you are in your 30s and up.

This approach consists of investing around 50% of your money into bonds and 50% into index funds.

The power of investing in Bonds

A bond is a type of lending investment in which you loan money to an entity, typically a corporation or a government. The entity would usually borrow your money for a defined period of time at a fixed or variable interest rate. Bonds are used by private companies, states, sovereign governments, and municipalities to raise money and finance a variety of undertakings.

Bonds are considered to be a stable, conservative kind of an investment. Aggressive investors also choose bonds for diversification reasons. Bonds offer higher returns than bank savings accounts. Bonds also don't have the volatility you usually find in a stock market.

A bond is similar to a Certificate of Deposit. The difference between them is that bonds are securities that trade in the market with fluctuating rates.

Let's consider an example. You can purchase a bond issued by, say, Wal-Mart scheduled to mature in five years and offers, say, 5.25% interest. This means that for five years the company will be sending you interest on the bond. After the five years are up, the company will return you the full amount of your bond.

The worst that can happen to your bond investment is that the company you've lent money to would go bankrupt. If the company does go bankrupt, there's a chance that you will lose both your original investment and the remaining interest payments.

However, bonds issued by businesses that have been operating for a long time, such as Wal-Mart, are usually very safe. On top of that, nobody is making you invest all your money in bonds of the same company. If you own bonds in a number of companies and one of them goes bankrupt, you will lose only a small portion of your total investment portfolio.

The difference between a bond and a Certificate of Deposit is that you can sell a bond anytime you need without incurring any penalties.

If you have a Certificate of Deposit, you usually need to commit to a certain period of time, usually 12 or 24 months. If you withdraw your money before the expiration date of the contract, you will usually incur a hefty fee that you don't have with bonds. On top of this, selling and buying shares of most bond mutual funds costs nothing, so you wouldn't even incur transactional fees when doing so.

There is one catch that you need to know about. Bonds pay higher returns than bank savings accounts and money market mutual funds because there's more risk involved. Bonds are riskier than the investment vehicles we just mentioned because their value can fall if interest rates go up. In addition to this, you do not have the FDIC insurance that Certificates of Deposit have.

At the same time, bonds tend to be a safer investment than stocks.

Bonds are a great long-term investment. Similarly to stocks, they can be sold any business day that the financial markets are open. However, the value of your bond will fluctuate. This means that if you absolutely need to sell your bond and the market is down, you will lose money. If you can wait and are in no rush to sell, you're very unlikely to lose money.

Here is another tip: don't put your saved money into bonds. That's what savings accounts and money market funds are for.

Here are some scenarios where investing in bonds makes great sense:

You are looking to make a big purchase a few years from now. In this case, shorter-term bonds are a little riskier than money market funds and CDs, but still a really safe investment.

You want to diversify your portfolio. Fluctuations in bond prices don't follow the changes in stock prices. In fact, in a really bad economic environment bond values may go up when stocks are taking a dive.

You are making strategic long-term investments for your retirement. As we've discussed in the previous chapter, investing in bonds doesn't make much sense for young aggressive investors. This being said bonds are a smart choice if you are nearing your retirement.

Bonds differ from one another based on a number of parameters – a number of years to maturity, credit rating and the entities that issue the bonds.

Maturity simply means the number of years when you will get your principal amount back. A bond's maturity date can give you an idea of how the value of the bond will change if the interest rates change. If interest rates go down, bond prices go up. If interest rates go up, bond prices go down. Longer-term bonds drop more in price when the interest rates go up compared to shorter-term bonds.

Let's take a look at an example. Suppose you are looking at two bonds from the same company. Both bonds yield 7% return. The only difference between the bonds is the maturity date. One bond matures in 2 years and the other one matures in 20 years. If interest rates go up just 1%, from 7% to 8%, the 2-year bond is likely to decline by about 2% in value. The 20-year bond is likely to decline 5 times as much – 10%.

The reason for bond prices falling when interest rates go up is very simple. If interest rates go up from 7% to 8%, the interest on similar bonds will rise to 8% and no one will be interested in buying your 7% bond. The value of your bond has to go down so that the bond effectively yields 8%.

Bonds are usually divided into groups based on their maturity date.

Short-term bonds mature in the next few years.

Intermediate-term bonds mature in 3 to 10 years.

Long-term bonds usually mature in 10+ years, generally up to 30 years.

Although very rare, there are bonds that have a maturity date of 100 years. IBM, Coca-Cola, Disney, the New York Port Authority and the government of China all have issued 100-year bonds at certain points. Obviously, these bonds are very risky investments, especially when you are buying them during a low-interest rate period.

Because of the higher risk, most of the time longer-term bonds pay better yields than short-term bonds.

In addition to differing in maturity, bonds also differ depending on the creditworthiness of the issuer. Credit-rating agencies such as Moody's, Fitch and Standard & Poor rate the quality and risk of default of bonds.

Credit rating depends on the ability of the bond issuer to pay back the debt. AAA is the highest rating. The ratings go down through AA and A, followed by BBB, BB, B, CCC, CC, C, DDD, DD, D and so on.

The bonds are considered to be high quality if they have a rating of AAA and AA.

If a bond has an A or BBB rating, it's considered to be of general quality.

Bonds with ratings below BBB are known as junk bonds. They are more likely to default compared to the bonds with higher ratings. A couple of percent of them actually do default every year.

Obviously, the lower the rating of the bond, the higher the risks, and the higher the yield percentages are.

Poorly rated bonds, however, are also more volatile in value compared to highly rated bonds.

Passive Investing

A mutual fund is a professionally managed investment fund that takes money from investors and pools it together for investment purposes. There is no strict legal definition of the term "mutual fund." The term is most often used to describe collective investment vehicles that are available to the general public. Hedge funds are not mutual funds because they are not sold to the general public.

An index fund is a type of mutual fund that has a portfolio designed to match or track the components of a market index, such as S&P 500.

Here is why investing in an index fund is a good idea: if you were to invest by yourself, you'd first have to pick the stocks you want to invest in. You probably don't know enough about the market to make such decisions. One of the rules of smart investing says: "Never invest in things you don't understand." Next, investing by yourself you'd be responsible for all the transaction fees.

Pulling the money together from different investors into a fund allows the fund to hire professional managers who can make smart investment decisions. These decisions bring in enough money to pay for fund personnel salaries and generate a nice return on investment.

Good index funds consist of stocks, bonds, and other assets the meet the fund's criteria. Such funds enable you to have some of the best investors in the country directly invest your money. Because efficient funds take most of the potential problems and costs out of deciding what stocks and assets to invest in, they are some of the best investment vehicles available to the general public.

Today investors have over $15 trillion invested in different mutual funds.

A huge benefit of an index fund is professional management. Usually, an index fund would hire a portfolio manager and researchers whose jobs are to find, analyze, predict and purchase investments for the fund. These people sort different investments and find those that meet the fund's goals.

Typically fund managers come to work for a fund after studying in the best finance and business schools in the country. Many pursue additional credentials, such as CFA (Chartered Financial Analyst).

Index funds are a cheap way of getting your investment research and decisions done. Often when you invest in an index fund, you pay less in transaction fees than you would pay if you were to trade securities on your own.

Funds also spread the cost of research over all their investors. The most efficiently managed index funds charge their members less than 1% per year in fees. Some of the largest funds charge even less – 0.2% per year. That's less than a $2 annual fee for every $1,000 that you invest.

One thing that makes index funds so attractive for investments is diversification. Most index funds purchase stocks from dozens of companies, minimizing the risk from any single company or sector of the market. Accomplishing the same level of diversification on your own would be very difficult and expensive.

While most index funds are really well-diversified, diversification is not a legal requirement. There are index funds that invest exclusively in a certain industry (healthcare being a great example) or country (such as Brazil). Be sure to check how well diversified the fund is before you invest in it.

Most index funds have very low investment minimums. Many have a minimum of $1,000 or less. If you want to open a retirement account, you can often invest even less than $1,000. Some index funds even offer monthly plans that start as low as $50 per month.

There are three kinds of index funds:

Stock funds heavily invested in stocks. This is the way to go if you are looking for a place where your money will grow over a longer period of time

Bond funds focus on investing in bonds. A bond fund is for you if you need current income and want less risk than you have with stock funds.

A money market fund is a fund that heavily invests in short-term debt securities, such as US Treasury notes. This is the way to go if you want to be sure that your invested principal doesn't go down in value and you may need your money back in the near future.

Most intelligent investors choose a combination of these types of funds to accomplish different financial goals.

As you well know, a lot of banks and financial institutions have gone bankrupt in the last decade.

Here's how banks and insurance companies work: customers give them money, which may need to be returned on a short notice. A bank would then invest or lend this money. If a bank lends a lot of money to untrustworthy institutions and customers and the loans go sour, the bank may go bankrupt.

This can't happen in an index fund because the value of a fund's share changes as the assets in the fund change in value. The worst-case scenario with an index fund is that if you want your money back, you may get less money than originally invested due to a market value decrease of the fund's assets – but you won't lose your initial investment.

Often for added security index funds hold specific stocks, bonds and other securities at a custodian. A custodian is a separate organization independent of the index fund. A custodian makes sure that an index fund doesn't embezzle your funds.

You can open an account with an index fund without even leaving your home. You can file a simple online form, provide your banking information for electronic transfers and the fund will take care of everything else for you.

Selling your shares in an index fund is also really easy. All you need to do is call the company or visit their website.

Conclusion

This book has covered everything you need to know about investing not only your finances but also your time, energy and other resources. Yes, it was a lot of information. However, it was important for us to cover each topic in detail to make sure you had all the necessary information available to you to implement investment strategies in your life. Investing can be risky and tricky, but it doesn't have to be terrifying. It also doesn't have to equal to gambling.

The ability to know what you want to invest your time in and how you want to spend your resources is one of the most important abilities you'll ever have in life because having this ability means that you can enjoy life and not worry about your savings, nest egg, and retirement.

This is why in the section about investing in your 20s we talked about IRAs, Roth IRAs and 401k. Investing in these vehicles is always a smart decision. However, the 20s should be more than just investing money. When you are young you want to travel and have various experiences and that's exactly what you should do.

As you get older, dividing your investments between bonds and index funds is the best method to achieve stable inflation-proof returns in any market conditions. This is why we devoted a whole chapter to bonds and index funds and explained all the pros and cons of investing in both. We also gave you plenty of examples and covered scenarios that show different outcomes for different kinds of investments.

Investing should be a pleasant process of gradually moving towards the accomplishment of your financial goals without major setbacks occurring on the way. Tools that we described in this book will help you create this kind of fulfilling, pleasant and productive investment experience.

We really appreciate you investing your time into reading this book. We hope it was very useful to you. If the knowledge, information, and tips shared in these pages help you on your path of growth and protection of your hard-earned savings and other resources, we've achieved our goal in writing this book.

BONUS- THE SMART PASSIVE INCOME (CHAPTER 1-2)

Introduction

Earning a passive income is something that a lot of people dream of. We all have heard myths about how we can easily make a lot of money without having to do a lot of work. We will jump all into products or programs people advertise online and hope that everything is just going to work out for the best. With this kind of mentality, we will end up failing pretty quickly. It is not the fact that making passive income is impossible; it is more the fact that most people who are drawn to this idea are not prepared for the time, investment and work that they need to put in.

This guide is a wakeup call to those who are looking to make a passive income. It is not necessarily meant to scare you away from attempting to earn one, but rather it is intended to tell you the truth and to let you know what it actually takes to achieve success. Many people think of passive income as an easy stream of money that they will not have to do much to get. While you can make some good money in the process, it is a lot of work and will continue to be a lot of work. This guidebook discusses this in some detail and is meant to educate you before you decide to take the plunge on this exciting income source.

This guidebook will inform you about the mindset of those who are able to work successfully with passive incomes. There are a lot of people who are able to make a passive income work and they never have to go back to a "9 to 5" job again. On the other hand, there are those who are just trying to make a quick buck and who do not want to put in the work. They are the ones who are the most likely to fail. To prepare you for success, this guidebook explains what a passive income is, who can make a passive income and some of the traits of those who are successful in making a passive income.

There are many common thoughts and misconceptions surrounding the notion of passive income. Most people think that having a passive income means that they have an easy job. They believe that they will make a ton of money without having to do much work. These thoughts are wrong and those who believe that are often the first to fail. For this reason, this book is intended to give you a realistic picture of what working for a passive income is like.

Earning a passive income is hard work and will require a lot of effort and time from the individual. To be successful, you have to be ahead of the curve and able to think outside the box in order to achieve the great benefits that you are anticipating. However, a passive income is not always just about hard work; there are a lot of benefits that you will be able to get if you are just willing to put in the effort. As well as being realistic about the challenges of earning a passive income, this guidebook also describes some of the benefits of this mode of money-making, such as being your own boss, having the potential to make a lot of money, more time with family, and more flexibility in hours.

Simultaneous to all of these delightful perks, there are some pitfalls of making a passive income. By explaining some of the pitfalls that you may experience with a passive income, such as losing money, losing the steady paycheck that you were used to in the beginning, and not having health insurance and other benefits, this book aims to make you prepared for these potential problems. You need to be informed about why a passive income can be dangerous and why you cannot take the term too literally, or you will lose out on all of your business.

Building a passive income business is a difficult process, and this book will help guide you through this in a practical and helpful way. If you have decided that you are up for the challenge and are still excited about this opportunity, then this book has the tools to kick off your new venture. You will need to do some research, such as knowing market demands and choosing the business that you would like to work with. You need to do this with the capability of sticking with it for the long term. This book will introduce you to some of the popular passive income markets where you will be able to make some good money, such as Kindle publishing, YouTube videos, and even blogging.

In order to give you some ideas about where to start, this book also includes the top 5 passive income options that are currently out there. These are options that have a lot of potentials to help you to take control of your life. Some options that are discussed in this chapter include: peer to peer lending, selling an informational product, and dividend investing. Being informed about these popular choices will give you a real basis for making your own decisions about your passive income business.

A passive income source is a great way for you to make some good money, but it is not as easy as you may have been told. Many companies will try to take your money and promise you the moon, but you have to be able to put in the time and effort in order to make it big. This guidebook is not meant to scare you away from the idea of making a passive income. Rather, it is intended to help you to have all of the information you need, and to be prepared so you actually stand a chance in order to make a great income with this source. Use the information in this guidebook in order to make the right decisions and get started on the right path to passive income today.

CHAPTER 1:

Do what Successful people do

Making a passive income is something that many people dream about. They have heard stories about how passive income earners are able to just sit back and make money with very little work. And this is where a lot of people end up getting stuck; they believe these stories and are not prepared for all of the actual work they need to put in to make the money they want. This first chapter is going to spend some time exploring the idea of passive income, explaining who can make a passive income, and identify some of the traits that you will find in those who are successful in making a passive income.

What is Passive Income?

To start this guidebook, we need to look at what exactly a passive income is in order to understand what is being discussed. A passive income is one that is received on a pretty regular basis, but one that is not going to require as much effort in order to maintain it. This does not mean that no work is going to be involved and, especially in the beginning, you will be putting in more work than many people do for their regular incomes; you will also be taking a big risk. And even when the income is secured, you will still need to put in the work. Many people think that passive incomes just involve a few hours of work and that is it for them to start making their millions. This is where they are going to fail and run into issues because they are not prepared for all of the hard work. At the same time, a passive income is different from a regular income in the sense that the money is not earned through your constant, active participation in a particular form of labor or service.

According to the IRS, passive income is defined as coming from just two sources, even though it is possible to earn it from other sources as well; these are just categorized under other sources when it comes to tax time. The two sources are trade activities in which the person does not materially participate and from the rental activity. Other governmental institutions recognize passive income as the income that is obtained with capital growth. Either way, the money you make from passive income is still going to be taxable just like other income sources you come across.

There are many different types of income that could be classified as passive income. Some examples include:

- Any income that you make off of your property. This could include rent from apartments, several units, or even your home; farming; or leasing out your land.

- Earnings that you might get from a business where you are not directly involved as the owner. You might own the business, but someone else is running the business and dealing with its day-to-day running.

- The interest that you make from your bank account. Usually, this is not going to be high enough to be taxable because you will be lucky if you make a few dollars from the transaction. There are a few banks that offer higher rates and if you invest wisely, it is possible to make more.

- Royalties—this can be from a patent, publishing a book, making a software product or other intellectual property, or even writing a song. You might have put in the work to produce the piece, but you are not actually doing work while the money is being made, so it is considered passive income.

- Earnings from posting advertisements. This is kind of a confusing one. To do this you need to own a website where interesting stories, pictures, and other information are posted. If you have a large enough following, other businesses may pay you to put an advertisement about them up. You will have to keep up the content of your website, but you will not be doing any work on the advertisements, so you are making a passive income.

- The interest comes from sources such as bonds or stocks. These can offer you a lot of good income if you make good choices about them, but there is always the possibility that you might suddenly lose a lot of money in the process as well.

Any of these can be considered passive income. As you can see, you are still going to need to put in quite a bit of work in order to make this kind of income. Yes, you can make money off of royalty checks, but you would have to put in the work to write a book, find a publisher, and market the book in order to make any money. You can make a good income from rental properties, but you have to worry about filling the buildings, cleaning them, upkeep, and going around and purchasing new properties if you would want more income. It is all going to take some work! Overall, it is the method of getting the money, as well as what happens when you get the money, that will determine if it is a passive income or not.

Who Can Make Passive Incomes?

In all honesty, anyone can make a passive income, but a lot of people are just not suited to the risk, hard work, and the time that needs to be committed in order to be successful. Many people who attempt to earn a passive income find that they fail with it because they are just not prepared to do the work or invest the money. They think that just a little bit of their time will be sufficient in order to get the money that they deserve so that they can go sailing around the world and live the life of the rich and famous. While this is a nice little dream, it really is not a reality.

The people who make a good living on passive incomes are the ones who are willing and ready to put in the hard work that is required. They are not the ones who sit back and expect the money to just be handed to them, and they are not the ones who will be duped into giving up all of their money by flashing lights and a lot of big words on a webpage. They are the ones who can think outside the box to the bigger picture, who will put in the work, and who will take the chances that no one else is willing to take in order to make a good income. They are also the ones who realize that they are never going to be able to take a break from their work, but that the reward, as well as the freedom, is so worth it. Theoretically, anyone could be like this, but the truth is that most people are either not hard enough workers, have trouble thinking critically, or just do not have the ambition to get the work done in order to make the passive income that they are looking for.

How Successful People Make Passive Incomes

So now that you know a little bit more about passive incomes, you might be curious to find out who the people are that are able to successfully earn money in this way. It sounds like such a great idea, but if it were so easy to do, then everyone would be on the bandwagon hoping to make their millions. And while many people do try to get a passive income, most of them are not ready for all of the work entailed in order to be successful. When they hear about passive income, they think that they will just put in a few hours of work and then sit back while the money just rolls in. As explained above, this is just not the way that these things work, no matter how much we might wish it was. This section will look at some of the key character traits and mindsets of those who earn a successful passive income.

Go-Getters

The first trait that you will notice in successful passive earners is that they are go-getters. They are not the kind of people who just sit there on the job and hope that good things will come their way, or complain when things go wrong. They are the ones who are out there getting their hands dirty, who like to work, and who are able to take control when opportunity strikes. Earning this kind of income is sometimes scary at the beginning for a lot of people because it is not always guaranteed. Many people might not like working for a boss they do not like, but they do like the predictability that comes with going to work each day and bringing home a reliable paycheck that can help support their family. This is not something that can be promised with a passive income.

This is a part of the tradeoff. Yes, you have to give up some of the predictability that you love with your regular income, but with some hard work you might be able to bring in a lot more money than you would from your old job, plus you get to be your own boss. There might be a lot of strange hours, but you would have more control over them and could make it to the big games or the concerts that you used to miss due to work. Even though the possibilities might seem wonderful, it is a big risk for a lot of people and it does not always pan out the way that it is promised. This is what keeps people at their regular jobs doing the same thing over and over again.

For those who are ready to jump in and get a passive income, this is a risk that is worth taking. They want to see the big rewards and are not worried about the risk as much as others. They will see the opportunity and they will jump right at it. They know that they will achieve the success that they want as long as they keep working hard and follow the right leads.

Independent Workers

If you are not able to work on your own without a lot of guidance and hand-holding along the way, you will find that a passive income method is not the right way for you to make money. When you are working to make a passive income, you are pretty much your own boss. This means that you do not have someone breathing down your neck telling you when the due dates are and where you need to be. You get to choose the hours and the work. Some people like this and others will find that they are lost and do not know what they are doing. If you are one of the latter, you should really stay away from this kind of work because those who are not able to keep themselves motivated and working hard will not be successful with this method.

There are some pros and cons to this kind of income source. First, you will be making your own money and will not have to share the credit with anyone else. This is appealing to some people who are tired of doing all of the work for a boss who takes all of the credit. You will also be able to keep all of the money that you earn without someone else dipping into your pockets. The issue is that when a mistake is made, you will be the one who is to blame and you will not be able to share that blame with someone else. To some people, this is hard to do and so they would rather just stick with their current job.

Passion

You have to love what you are doing and the freedom that it can give you if you are looking to be someone who is successful at passive incomes. Anyone who is looking to be an entrepreneur is going to be really passionate about the things that they are doing and this is a big reason that they are so successful in their work. When you are passionate about something, you are more likely to work hard at it. You want to see how far you can take it and you will always be able to find something new and exciting that will draw you towards the work again. Those who are working with streams of passive income are going to have a lot of the same passions as other entrepreneurs since they will also be striking out on their own. The passion is the thing that is going to keep you moving forward, even when things get a little rough, you lose a little money, or when the work is not always that much fun.

Self-Motivated

When you are making your own passive income, you are not going to have a boss looking over your shoulder telling you what to do all of the time. You will not necessarily have clients who are telling you what they want to be done either. You are going to be the one who is in charge of getting the work done. While you may not get in trouble if you forget to do something or don't finish the work, you will not make the money that you were hoping for and this can be just as bad.

Whether or not this is a problem is going to depend on the type of person you are. Some people love to be on their own and to be their own boss. They love how it feels when they get to do all of the work, figure things out for themselves, decide when they work and how much they make. They are motivated enough to keep on going through it all, even when they are unsure of how things will turn out. Other people might like the structure of having a boss. They might not be able to stay motivated without someone there to tell them how things work and where they should be all of the time. If you are one of the former, then making a passive income might be a smart move for you; if you are one of the latter, it is probably better if you stick with the job you are currently in.

Basic Computer Skill

This does not mean that you have to be an advanced IT person who can hack into any system and take over a government, but it sure is an advantage if you know your way around a computer and understands how it all works. The computer is going to be your best friend when it comes to making a passive income and if the idea of using one makes you break out in a sweat, it is probably best to stick with your 9 to 5 job or consider learning some computer skills. You should at least have some of the basic computer skills handy that you would have learned in school such as searching, composing notes, emailing, and browsing in order to get things started. Being able to build your own website and a few other advanced skills can also really help, depending on the form of passive income that you are going for. If you do not have any experience with using a computer, you are really putting yourself at a disadvantage.

Problem Solvers

When working for a passive income, there are going to be times when you will need to be able to get out of a tough situation and figure out the best solution. The issues that arise are going to depend on the kind of passive income stream you are going for. You need to not get caught up in the work or start to get anxious and worried when problems arise because this is not how you will get things done. When bad things happen, you need to be able to jump up and take care of the issue the best that you can before it gets any worse. If you are good at taking initiative and fixing issues in this way, then a passive income may be an ideal income source for you.

Can Predict the Trends

Those who are really successful in making a passive income are the ones who are able to predict what is going to happen next and what will be successful. Often those who fail at making a passive income do so because they are jumping on a trend that has actually been around for a while and money has already been made off of it. To be really successful, you need to be ahead of the game and to be able to see things in a new way in order to jump on new trends.

When it comes to many of the passive income options, it is pretty important that you are able to correctly predict how people are going to purchase things in the future and what a good idea looks like. For example, affiliate marketers might be able to guess what will sell the best over a few quarters and then make a profit, but if they guess wrong, they will lose out on making some good money. Take a look at the trends in the market that you are going into and decide what is most likely to happen in the future, so you can expand upon and make money from.

They Have Knowledge

Some of the people who go into passive income jobs will just naturally have a lot of knowledge, either in general or about the market they are trying to go into. This does not mean that you will not have success if you are not naturally gifted with prior knowledge. It is still possible to get some success in this stream by learning on-the-go. Either way, you need to have some knowledge in your field and to be able to see what is going to come in the future. You also need to be able to identify if something is a good idea or not. You should not be making a lot of guesses in the field you are choosing; while you might be able to get some lucky breaks, this is not a good way to run a business and you will find that you are ultimately going to fail in a big way. Sure, you might make some mistakes, but you should be working towards building your knowledge in such a way that these mistakes are minimal.

Before you get started on a new passive income stream, you should make sure to get as much information as possible about it. If you grew up around this kind of thing, such as having parents who rented out apartment buildings and you are going into rentals, you are at an advantage. If you do not have any past experience, get out there and learn as much as you possibly can. Read online, go visit the library, talk to someone in the field, look around at available apartments in your area, and pretty much do anything that you can think of to become an expert in the field.

These are just a few of the traits that are noticeable in the people who choose to go into passive income fields. It is a great way to make some money and be your own boss, but it is not always as easy as the advertisements and other people might try to lead you to believe. You will have to have the right mindset, be willing to take some risks and be ready to put in the hard work to see success. If these personality traits sound like you now, or maybe the kind of person you are willing to put in the effort to become, then passive income may be the right choice for you!

CHAPTER 2:

The Truth about Passive Income

Many people have heard about passive incomes. They hear the stories about how people are able to become rich in no time and often they think that very little if any, work is involved. Honestly, these are the kinds of people who get taken advantage of when it comes to the passive income game and often they will be the ones who get in a lot of trouble and lose all of their money. These beliefs are prevalent in so many people that the market is becoming saturated with new people who are excited to make the money. However, since many of these people are not ready for the work and investment involved in earning a passive income, they will soon drop out and just those who are serious about the work will stick with it.

This chapter is going to talk about some of the common thoughts about passive income that most people have, but which are usually way off the mark. It will then go into some of the realities about passive income and the hard work that is involved in the process.

Common Misconceived Thoughts about Passive Income

As mentioned above, there are a lot of different thoughts that people have when it comes to earning a passive income. They may have heard some things from their friends or family about passive income. Often this information is from a friend of a friend, so it may not be based on first or even second-hand experiences. The fact is, this is actually better than the information many other people are going on; they might be relying on something they heard in a YouTube video or from a website about all of the benefits that come from passive income. This is dangerous because most of the claims made on these kinds of mediums are false. They lead you to believe the work is easy, but often they are just trying to take your money.

Because of all of the confusion about what passive income is and how it works, there are many notions about it that are false. This section is going to look at some of the misconceived thoughts about passive income that might be the reason why so many people fail when trying to gain one.

Easy

The first thought that most people have about passive incomes is that they are easy. This might be a combination of the things they have heard in the past, as well as connotations that are brought up by the name itself. Most people have the idea that when they are making a passive income, they will take a few hours to do the work, pay a little bit of money, and then they will be all set to make a lot of money for the rest of their lives without having to do anything else except receiving their checks each month. And this is the reason that so many of them get taken advantage of by the flashing lights on a website.

Passive income is more like an alternative way for you to make money. It does not mean that you will not be working in order to get money; you just will not be going to a traditional 9 to 5 job in order to get a paycheck. You have to be able to multi-task, problem solves, and see trends in the market in order to get ahead of the game and keep the money coming in all of the time. The work will never be done—this is another reason that a lot of people fail. They are not ready for the risk, the dedication, and the time that they have to put into the entire process in order to make it big. Learn from their mistakes and you will have a much better chance of success.

Very Profitable

One reason that a lot of people will get into passive income is that they think they will be able to make a lot of money in a very short amount of time. While it is possible to make some good money with a passive income, it is not going to be something that will make you a million dollars overnight. It is something that will take you a lot of time and effort before you can even make a little bit of money. In fact, you might find that you will need to invest some of your own money to even get to that point.

It is important to remember that you need to be careful about what you are investing your money in when trying to earn a passive income. Yes, there are times that you will need to input some money to make a profit, but this does not mean you should not think it through and just hand out money left and right. For example, if you stumble across a website that you have never heard of which promises to give you the secrets to making millions a month if you just give them $200, you should probably stay away. They are just going to take your money and send you a video to convince you to send them more. They have found a good way to make a passive income by becoming rich off the desperation of others without being willing to put in the work like you are. On the other hand, if you want to start making a passive income on apartment buildings, you will have to put in some money to purchase a property, advertise the space, maintain it, and so on. Both situations involve money being spent at the outset, but one is going to make you money while the other is just going to lose your money.

If you are willing to put in the time and effort that is needed, it is possible to make a very good income by doing this. But it is not just going to happen overnight, and you will have to work quite a bit to achieve it. Plus, the work will continue and you will still have to show up and do something in order to make the passive income. For example, let's go back and look at the apartment income option. You cannot purchase the apartments, clean them up, fill the vacancies, and then walk away and still make money. You have to go in and fix things if they break, answer questions and complaints, keep it looking nice, and fill up vacancies when someone moves out. Or you could get away with not doing this work by hiring someone else or letting the apartments fall into disarray. However, choosing this option is just going to end up with you having empty apartments you cannot fill and which are a money pit.

As you can see, it is possible to make quite a bit of money from passive income, but it is not a get rich quick scheme and it is something you will actually need to work hard in order to achieve. However, it is a way to get some freedom and earn some financial success if you are able to do it in the correct way and work hard to get ahead.

Little Work

This is one of the areas where people are most likely to fail. They might be ready to dedicate some of the risk and some of the monetary investment, but they just are not ready to put in the time. They might have heard from someone that making a passive income is easy and that other than a few hours of work, they are not going to need to do anything for the paychecks to keep coming in. They think a passive income is a hobby or something they can just spend some time on when they want to. When they get to actually doing the work, they are amazed at the effort they really need to go through in order to make any money. In some cases, it's much less money than they were promised.

There is a lot of work that will need to be done in order to actually make the income you are looking for. It is not as easy as you might like and you will find that it might even be harder than the work you are doing. Plus, with the risks so high, you may not be able to make the same kind of money. It takes a certain kind of person and a certain kind of situation in order to make it big with a passive income, and although it would be nice to just go home and have a big fat check waiting for you without having to do the work, it just is not a reality that most people get to live with. If you want to make the money, you have to do the work.

The Reality of Making Passive Income

As you can probably imagine by this point, the realities of making a passive income are not as nice and rosy as many companies would like you to believe. If you find a company that is offering to help you make an easy passive income or tell you that there will not be much work involved, it might be in your best interest to run the other way! Anyone who has actually done passive income and who is not trying to steal all of your money will be able to tell you that it is a lot of work and that you will need to put in the time and effort in order to make it all come together.

There are some realities that will come with making a passive income. Most people do not start to realize these until they have started on their project. Once they get started, they realize it is more work or money than they are willing and able to do or pay. Here are some of the crucial realities that come with making a passive income which you should know and understand before you get out there and start. These are not meant to put you off trying for a passive income. Rather, these tips are a way for you to understand what is actually going to happen with this stream of income so that you can get those thoughts of easy money out of your head. It is possible to make money, but it is not going to be handed to you. If you are not ready for the risk, investment, and hard work, it is better to know that ahead of time before it ends in heartache.

Some of the realities you should be prepared for when it comes to passive income include:

- It is not always easy — you will have to work hard in order to get the things that you want out of this source of income. The money is not going to be handed to you and you will not be able to sail away on your boat while others do all the hard work. If someone is telling you this, they just want to make money off you and you are the one financing their expensive trips all over the world. You have to be dedicated to the work and ready to put in the hours. Think of it as your own little business; you wouldn't expect the business to be done and earning money in a short amount of time, and neither will your stream of passive income.

- It is hard work — get ready for the long days and late nights. Unlike your regular job, there are no set hours and if something needs to be done, you have to take care of it. This is not a good venture for someone who just wants to be lazy or has things done for them. Sure, you can do it this way, but you probably will not be that happy with the results you get.

- There will be an investment — this can mean many different things. You may need to invest your time, your energy, your money, or all three. But please be careful where the money goes. Just because someone is asking for your money does not mean you will be given everything as promised.

- Risk — there are a lot of risks that come from making a passive income, and this is not always about the loss of money, although that could be a factor. It is risky to give up your current steady stream of income in order to make something happen. It is risky to give up the security you are used to, a job in this economy, and the health benefits or retirement fund you may have at your job. You may fail in the end; many people end up not seeing the results they were looking for. You have to realize that there is a risk in this kind of thing and without the right confidence and the right knowledge about the subject you may increase your risk of failure.

- The potential for high income — you may be able to make some good money from getting a passive income, but not everyone will.

Some people will back out before any money is spent. Others will lose a little bit of money in the process, while some will lose it all. Still, others are going to find that they are making a little bit of money but not really enough to give up their other jobs or to get far ahead. It is those lucky ones who are able to plan ahead and make things work that are going to be able to potentially make a lot of money from all of this. Making a good passive income is going to take work. It is not always going to come to everyone who tries, but it is something that can happen.

As you can see, the realities of a passive income are quite a bit different than the thoughts and notions most people have about it. As mentioned above, these are not meant to scare, but to give you have a clearer idea of what a passive income entails so that rather than relying on the wrong information given by others, you will be more prepared for the work and for making the decision on whether this is the right income stream for you to pursue in the first place.

Thank you for reading "The First Time Investor". If you like and find this book helpful. Please take some time to share your thoughts and post a review. It'd be greatly appreciated.

Remember: Success is 80% Mindset/20% Strategy

I wish you the best and good luck!

Bruce Walker

www.ingramcontent.com/pod-product-compliance
Lightning Source LLC
Chambersburg PA
CBHW060408080526
44583CB00012B/511